"George Selleck has called upon his attributes as a scholar and grandfather to author *Kian and Me: Gifts from a Grandson*, a heartwarming story about the very young teaching the very old. Toddler Kian's expressions and mannerisms infused new purpose into his grandpa, an octogenarian babysitter whose ailments and attitude experienced a healing affect in the therapeutic company of a special child. A beautifully told story, touching both the mind and the soul."

—**Dave Newhouse**, Columnist, Sportswriter, and Author

"Dr. George Selleck could have been a professional basketball player, but he chose to become a Presbyterian minister, pursue a PhD in counseling psychology, and devote his life to reminding young people—and their parents—that there is more to life than sports....Through it all, Selleck remained steadfast in his belief in the power of young people."

—**Aaron L. Miller**, PhD California State University, East Bay

"Dr. Selleck nails it in *Kian and Me*! What a fun and refreshing read of a most special relationship—the kind of which is open to so many of us, if we take the time to let it in. Unfortunately, we too often tend to think only of ourselves as 'the coach,' but there is an entire new generational world out there most of us can learn from if we make time to truly observe and listen! In summary, two-year-old Kian is a great teacher because his grandfather realized, if he himself listened, how much he could learn about appreciation of little, but valuable, things from someone more than eighty years his junior."

—**Dick Gould**, Vice Chairman, TeachAids; Emeritus, Men's Tennis Coach & Director of Tennis, Stanford University

"The first thing that crossed my mind after finishing George Selleck's *Kian and Me: Gifts from a Grandson* was pure envy that I had not written this marvelously poignant and insightful series of letters to my three young grandsons. Kian is too young to know how fortunate he is to have a grandpa (Papa) like George. But make no mistake, grandson Kian is at the heart of this book which leaves all of us with rare gifts of learning, sharing, growing old, growing young, and living fully."

—**Tom Meschery**, Author of *Sweat: New and Selected Poems about Sports*

"This is such a special piece, and so powerful in its quiet and calm demeanor. The way Selleck writes makes it seem like he is speaking gently into someone's ear from a cozy armchair next to a roaring fire, peacefully reflecting on life. It is such a wonderful demonstration of love and documentation of precious memories."

—**AnnMarie Baines**

"I love it. I cried, I laughed, I learned. It is George Selleck's absolutely best work. I could not put the manuscript down. Thank you for sharing it with us."

—**Lily Richardson**, PSA

KIAN and ME
GIFTS *from a* GRANDSON

By DR. GEORGE SELLECK

Post Hill
PRESS

A POST HILL PRESS BOOK
ISBN: 978-1-63758-109-4
ISBN (eBook): 978-1-63758-110-0

Post Hill Press
New York • Nashville
posthillpress.com

Published in the United States of America
1 2 3 4 5 6 7 8 9 10

To Barbara Grillo-Selleck, an incredible "Nana" and my wife, whose expertise, creativity, dedication, time, and effort in her relationship with Kian is something to behold. It has been my privilege to enjoy this grandparenting journey at her side

To Beth Hahn, the mother of my three kids, there is not enough praise in the world for how you raised our children and helped them become such wonderful people nor enough words for me to express my gratitude

TABLE OF CONTENTS

FOREWORD

It's difficult to find a more powerful and poignant collection of life advice than George's warm and heartfelt letters to his grandson, Kian.

Mark Twain once observed that the two most important days in one's life are the day one is born onto this earth and the day one discovers why.

That observation has always stayed with me in my own personal journey. But as George Selleck, aka Papa, writes so eloquently, one's life odyssey is filled with all sorts of everyday pleasant experiences that we too often take for granted. Whether he's sharing his thoughts on the act of enjoying pure play, learning from one's mistakes, coping with unexpected changes and challenges, developing true and dependable friendships, or growing and maturing into a true leader, *Kian and Me: Gifts from a Grandson* is an amazingly compact and concise compendium of timeless and universal advice.

George relies on his lifetime work of having studied the writing of top psychologists, philosophers, educators, and even humorists to help Kian find his own path. Of course, Kian was only two when this book was first published. But as he grows up, like the strong and sturdy oak tree that George refers to, this is a volume that should always be kept close at hand; indeed, it's an essential read for any parent or grandparent who is eager to find some trusted guidance on the ongoing mystery we call life.

As someone who just recently became a grandparent for the first time myself, I find George's words resonate deeply and provide real comfort and personal direction. His chapters are to be read slowly and carefully, digested word by word, and phrase by phrase. The truth is, lots of parents attempt to provide written words of wisdom for their next generation, and they are to be genuinely saluted. But George's words are different. They are timely, impactful, and full of all the wisdom he has gathered from his own extraordinary and amazing life.

We all know that our days on this planet are finite and limited, and that we are going to have our ups and downs along the way. But what a gift it is to have this stellar work of insights to gently guide us in our relationships with our children's children.

Rick Wolff

Senior Executive Editor

Houghton Mifflin Harcourt Publishing

January 2021

INTRODUCTION

There's an Albert Schweitzer quote that has always been a favorite of mine. A humanitarian and physician as well as a Nobel Peace Prize winner, Schweitzer believed strongly that we all had an ethical obligation to help others. He understood, better than most, the value of life and the importance of human connection. One of his most recognized quotes is, "At times our own light goes out and is rekindled by a spark from another person. Each of us has cause to think with deep gratitude of those who have lighted the flame within us."

When my grandson, Kian, was born, my light was—to put it bluntly—going out. In my eighties, diagnosed with Chronic lymphocytic leukemia (CLL) followed by a malignant and invasive melanoma tumor and severely blocked arteries, I was fighting a losing battle with ever-surmounting medical challenges.

Those haven't changed. But my outlook has. Tasked with watching Kian for the "morning shift" when he was first born, I marveled at his unassuming and easily offered grin, his growing curiosity, his contentment at just "being." My amusement morphed into reflective gratitude as I began to understand the many lessons I could learn from this tiny new human.

I've spent much of my life promoting youth leadership, encouraging kids to find meaning and enjoyment through athletics, and trying to inspire others to live healthy, active lives. More recently, I founded a program called *Lead2Play*. Through *Lead2Play*, young people are given the opportunity to be in charge of creating fun and meaningful sports and fitness experiences. More than that, though, this program is the culmination of my life's commitment to student self-advocacy and youth empowerment.

When presented with a challenge on how to lead, educate, or motivate young people, I have a simple, but oft-repeated mantra: "Ask the children." Given the tools, support, encouragement, and feedback they need, young people are so much more capable of "figuring it out" than we often give them credit for.

In watching Kian grow from infant to toddler, I was reminded again to "ask the children." Kian's unending curiosity, his willingness to fall and fail and get right back up, his positivity, his leadership, and the connection I felt with him all inspired me to both self-reflect on my own life—successes and failures alike—and marvel again how much we can learn from our youngest generation.

Empowerment, at its core, means "to give power to" someone. On a deeper level, it means to promote the self-actualization of someone. In observing and spending time with Kian, I realized how easily we "empower" our infants and toddlers. "Go on," we urge them. "Try that toy; taste that food; look at that book; say that word." We expect them to try to put the round block in the square hole. "Keep trying," we say. "You'll get it." When words aren't pronounced correctly, we model and encourage but give them the time and space they need to figure it out on their own.

Watch any parent eager for their baby to walk. You'll see empowerment—interspersed of course with the normal array of flinches, gasps, and cringes as that child inevitably teeters off-balance and falls. "You'll get it. Keep trying," we say. Because how else will that sweet child learn to walk otherwise?

If only we—collectively, as a society—continued empowering our kids as they aged. When they get a math problem wrong, when they strike out in baseball, when they don't pass their driver's test, when they need to figure out how they learn best, when they have a test to study for—what if we behaved as if they were learning to walk again? What if we empowered them to—with faith and support and love and assurances—know with certainty that they are capable of completing the task before them and equally as capable of surviving the fallout if they don't?

In the two years he's been alive, Kian has taught me many things and reminded me of many others. He's empowered me—to address some of my shortcomings, to give myself grace, to challenge me to be a better version of myself. Just as I hope I have empowered him to explore his world, take risks, ask questions, solve problems.

He has rekindled my spark. And my gratitude to him for that is deep.

CHAPTER ONE
The Gift of Connection

October 2020

Dear Kian,

It is your Papa writing to you. I imagine that you will read this someday when you are older. Maybe in the last months of high school or perhaps the summer before you start college, you'll sit down and read these letters and know the incredible impact you had on your grandfather.

Right now, though, you are an active and adorable toddler—just twenty-one months old. Yes! Just three months short of your second birthday on January 17, 2021. It is a tumultuous world you enter—an unprecedented time of insecurity and anger, of hardship and division.

As I write this, we are an anxious and fearful nation. The world is fraught with economic uncertainty and concern for the health of our planet and its inhabitants. A pandemic caused by a virus known as COVID-19 is infecting millions of people across the globe. Too many people have already lost their lives to this virus, and doctors fear that more will succumb to it before a vaccine can make its way into enough people's arms to successfully stop its spread. In just a few weeks, a decisive national election will take place that, while welcomed by many, may deepen the political and social divisions in our nation. Voters worry increasingly about their own family's health, the education of their children, and loss of jobs and careers.

It is also a challenging time for your papa. I, too, have fears for my health. I am currently battling two cancers. Because of this, I have regular chemotherapy treatments for Chronic lymphocytic leukemia. I also was recently forced to have a surgery to remove an invasive melanoma tumor. As if that were not enough to make your papa weary, a sobering conversation with a cardiologist sent me to the hospital with near total blockage in one artery and moderate to severe problems in the others. A large stent saved me from bypass surgery. But this most recent health issue has taken its toll on me in many ways.

I share all of this with you, Kian, so you'll understand why I write these letters to you. I am eighty-six years old. My body is telling me to slow down, which is no surprise. Lifelong friends of mine are already gone. It is a daily struggle to battle the fatigue and weariness that has set in. But my mind is as alert as ever, for better or worse.

I've often been labeled a "worrywart." I'm prone to anxiety and, too easily, I allow stress and tension to overshadow accomplishment and joy. However, the mental anguish of these last months is deeper and more profound than anything I have experienced before in my life. The questions I ask myself frequently about my life and its meaning are not easily ignored nor answered. I have had to admit that I am not sure I truly know myself as a human being.

Sharing this information—especially with a cherished grandson—is difficult. But this is the context in which you came into my life. In the months surrounding your birth, I was preoccupied by failure: failure to put aside unreasonable expectations for myself and what I'm still capable of accomplishing; failure to understand how to balance my aspirations with my deteriorating health; failure to overcome lingering guilt.

I will confess to having an annoyingly loud and persistent inner critic. It's one that has unfortunately plagued me for nearly the entirety of my life but has grown louder in recent months. This critic is ruthless. It knows precisely when to strike and how to quickly convince me that there must be something inherently wrong with me. This ever-present critic, and the subsequent feelings of worry, guilt, anxiety, depression, and self-doubt, have often prevented me from conquering my inner demons and becoming the best version of myself. Psychotherapist and author Sheldon Kopp may have summarized my predicament most succinctly: "All of the significant battles are waged within the self." I'm engaged in this fight with no plans to surrender.

I'll admit that, after more than eight decades, I am still a work in progress, in part because of your being here. I am still working to embrace my flaws, to accept who I am, and quit chasing an image that is not only unrealistic but unfulfilling.

I suppose that most grandfathers would use this time and platform to share advice and wisdom with their grandsons. But that is not my purpose. In fact, quite the opposite.

So, what *is* the goal of these letters? I don't wish to impart wisdom, nor bemoan the struggles that plague me and our world. My hope is, in a nutshell, to share the gifts you've given me in the short months that you've been alive.

Kian, I hope you won't mind if I spend a few minutes talking about your very early life and the start of our relationship. You were born prematurely. You came home the day following your birth to a house near mine on Brian Street in Tara Hills. Despite constant communication and assurance from your doctor, it was hard not to worry.

Shortly after your birth, I remember running into a kind woman who swam in the lane next to me each morning at 6:00 a.m. at the local YMCA. I told her about you, about my concerns. She unabashedly shared that she had raised a premature baby boy who ended up playing football and weighing over 250 pounds.

"He'll be fine," she reassured me every morning. "He just needs extra care right now."

Though your home was within walking distance of mine, I never made that walk. I met you on the second, or maybe the third, day of your life. You were tiny and needed round-the clock care. Having been an early riser my entire life, I offered to take the first shift of each day, which usually started at 5:30 or 6:00 and lasted a couple of hours.

So, every morning, I held you in my arms, marveled at your existence, and did everything I could to keep you comfortable. Your world-class smile had not yet arrived. But to me, you were already irresistible.

In retrospect, I don't really know why I volunteered to do those morning shifts. Maybe because I was always awake anyway. Maybe because I wanted to help, and this was one way to do that. I knew that caring for you those first few weeks would be a daunting task for new parents. I think I hoped to share in that burden.

Except it was never a burden. In many ways, in fact, you took care of me. You held me tightly. You squeezed my hand in your tiny one. You taught me lessons that I had failed to learn in over eighty-six years.

That is why I write these letters. I hope you can indulge your papa as I seek to share with you the importance of our connection—this new relationship, friendship even, with you—that has somehow allowed me to embrace who I am and let go of this idealistic and unattainable idea I've had of who I thought I was supposed to be. Those mornings with you, and the connection I felt with you, almost immediately helped me move closer to a better version of myself.

Thank you, Kian. For inspiring and guiding me through the most difficult time of my life. Thank you for being here, in your springtime of life, when I—in my winter—needed you the most.

Many years ago, I was introduced to the difference between childlikeness and childishness. To be childlike is to possess and exhibit enthusiasm and directness, simplicity and trust, an unfailing appetite for what's next, and a joy for life. It is to have an unending sense of wonder. To be childish on the other hand, is to be silly or immature. Basically, it is to exhibit the more unfavorable qualities of youth.

Kian, I now recognize childlikeness and child-ishness in my life at almost every stage. I believe that maturity means we grow out of childishness, but we never lose our childlikeness. As a toddler, you were beautiful and delightful in every way—the epitome of childlike! My fervent hope is that you will carry that childlike spirit all the days of your life.

Love,

Papa

CHAPTER TWO
The Gift of Play

November 2020

Dear Kian,

Like most toddlers, you are a master of play. Watching you play, day after day, has been one of the greatest experiences of my life. At its core, your play was generally about having fun and finding enjoyment. Watch any child tear through a playground or run around a park, and you will undoubtedly hear their screams of laughter and delight. Play is inherently fun. And if something is fun, we're more likely to do it willingly and happily.

But as fun as play is, we shouldn't dismiss the act of playing as insignificant and meaningless. Experts have long known the benefits of play. Ask any psychologist, learning specialist, teacher, or pediatrician and they'll argue that having fun—that playing—boosts learning potential. Playing actually makes us smarter.

Gradually, though, as I watched you play, I truly began to understand just how significant play really is in shaping how children see the world. Through play, you were learning and developing ideas about how the world worked. Playing was helping you think critically, problem solve, and practice how to be a leader. It strengthened your joy of learning. Yes, play was fun, joyful, and sometimes silly. But to dismiss your play as only fun and games would be to undermine its importance: it was the fundamental way you were learning and developing socially.

When you were still just learning to walk, your parents, always wise, noticed the limitations of your too-small Brian Street house. As you progressed from infant to toddler, and your parents began working from home, it became evident that you were all outgrowing the house that you had first come to as a baby. So, your parents bought a much bigger home on Longhorn Street about four miles from our condo.

Your new home was a two-story house on a hill. The four upstairs rooms became bedrooms for you and

Mommy and Daddy, which left two for their offices. The downstairs was unremarkable: a rather small kitchen and a cramped family room that could hold little more than a couch and TV. However, there was a large living room area that was set aside to be your play area.

And what a lovely playroom it was! There was a low flat futon on the floor that was perfect for sitting and playing. There was enough space for tunnel- and fort-making using cloth and wire. A set of low shelves held dozens of books and manipulatives. It was set against a wall of windows that overlooked bushes and colorful flowers and a street full of interesting noises and activity to observe.

Everywhere were places for baskets, which were quickly filled with puzzles, building blocks, shapes, and clever boxes with slots for each shape. One basket held only colorful foam letters and numbers. Another had brightly-hued pom-poms. Still more baskets had Velcro cutouts of food, balls of all sizes, spinners, and colored cars. A tiny basketball hoop in the corner stood ready for your pudgy arms to thrust a ball into it.

An Old MacDonald tractor brimmed with farm animals ready to prompt you to "Moo!" and "Neigh!" and "Bawk!" And your wise mama even included a stand with child-sized cleaning tools: a broom, a dustpan, and a mop. Should that array of toys fail to interest you, there was also a large yard that invited plenty of fun outdoor exploration and water activities.

Each day, I watched, fascinated, as you tested out your ideas about the world with these toys. Through these objects, your interactions with people, and a constant stream of new and interesting situations, you developed valuable skills, including physical, social, emotional, cognitive, and language skills. This learning wasn't mandated or prescribed. Instead, it was fostered by curiosity, interest, and a never-ending quest to play.

Kian, let me say it again: Even as I struggled with aging and battled a debilitating illness, even as feelings of oppressive anxiety persisted and lifelong issues of identity and meaning festered, I found immense delight in watching you spend most of your waking hours playing. Your brain and body got stronger. You learned how to have fun. You discovered how to avoid boredom by moving to another activity. Play, in all of its many forms, created lots of opportunities for your growth.

As play fostered your learning, watching you play was providing a sort of education for me as well. I'd never questioned the importance of play in a child's life. But it was like I was suddenly seeing firsthand just how great an impact it truly has.

First and foremost, it became abundantly clear that play is about enjoyment. Play should be fun and joyful. By definition, play should not feel onerous or burdensome.

Second, play is about the experience, or the process, and not the performance. In your playtime, you were engaged in lifting, dropping, looking, pouring, bouncing, hiding, knocking things down, building them back up, and more. You played for no other reason than it made you happy. It didn't seem to have a particular purpose. And that was an epiphany for me: Play does not need—in fact, should not have—a defined purpose.

I remember on one occasion when Nana brought you a bunch of measuring jars. We watched you—entranced ourselves—as you were totally self-absorbed in the task of pouring water from one jar to the next, over and over. You had no desire to achieve a particular result. Your goal was to joyfully engage in and master a process: learning how to pour water.

My experience with play was much different. Play, for me, was focused on performance. It was always about not embarrassing myself, impressing others, overcoming self-doubt, improving certain skills, and trying to win. Did I have fun? Rarely. Was it enjoyable? Sure, if we won. But to play simply to enjoy the process of playing? This was as foreign to me as trying to "win" at pouring water would have been to you.

One of the most powerful lessons you are teaching me as you play is that the process of playing is the driving value of your experience—not the performance or the outcome. Kian, I was an accomplished athlete. In 1952, I was selected as the state of California's High School Basketball Player of the Year. This was after I successfully led my Compton High School team to a 32-0 record and a championship victory. I fielded basketball scholarship offers from colleges spanning the country; I had my pick of schools. I played for Stanford and earned my place in the Stanford Basketball Hall of Fame. I was inducted into the Pac-12 Hall of Honor. At age seventy-eight, I took part in a full-court, five-on-five international basketball championship in Brazil—a game which I helped my team win.

But not once in my athletic career do I remember feeling a sense of joy about having a ball in my hands, having teammates to play with, or having the health and vitality to run, jump, shoot, and score. I was a serious guy. Basketball was serious stuff. I failed to see how it was fun.

Thanks to you, Kian, I see that and so many things differently. Your inspiration and example are helping me identify and address my misunderstandings regarding play. With you and watching you, I am simply having fun. I enjoy the moment. It's not easy to overcome a lifetime's reputation of being the "serious guy" and a worrywart. But Kian, I am trying. Thanks to you, I'm making progress, too.

I'll end this letter with a wonderful story that comes to mind. A simple activity on a nondescript day that taught me a lot about the importance of play as a source of fun, joyfulness, and connecting with people. We were in your backyard. As usual, you were enthralled with the most mundane of things. On this day, it was the rocks, sticks, and leaves that were scattered across the ground.

As I watched, bemused, you would pick up a rock, or a leaf, or maybe a stick. With a mischievous grin, you would act as if you were going to eat it. Being the protective Papa, I could not let this happen, of course.

"No, no, Kian," I would say, shaking my head and arms to discourage you. Mine was not an angry tone or manner, which I assume you ascertained from the sheepish grin that would creep across your face. Eventually, you grew tired of our wonderful game. However, the fun and enjoyment of sharing those silly, seemingly meaningless moments with you lives on in my memory.

Which leads me to a monumental revelation: Playtime and play areas are not just for children. Adults—in fact, all humans—need time to play to recreate ourselves through play. What a gift to finally understand this in the winter of my life. I strive each day to be more and more like you, to be fun loving, playful, and to embrace my own sense of humor.

Kian, I hope I can continue to be inspired by your play! I see how it energizes you, lifts you out of boredom, calms you, and opens you up to new possibilities. I have lived on this earth for eight decades, but never before have I wanted so much to joyously throw myself into new experiences, let my imagination run wild, and to play like a child. You have convinced me that play is, indeed, the gateway to vitality, and that we all need to play.

Thank you,

Papa

CHAPTER THREE
The Gift of Curiosity

November 2020

Greetings Kian,

Merriam-Webster (who I hope is still around when you read this) defines the word *curious* as "marked by desire to investigate and learn." A second definition, however, is slightly less favorable: "marked by inquisitive interest in others' concerns." Like Webster, society seems rather indecisive about curiosity. Curious George was always finding himself in trouble. Curiosity is known to cause the demise of the poor cat. Yet, revered creators such as Walt Disney, Stephen Hawking, and Albert Einstein all implore us to be eternally curious.

Perhaps we can find wisdom from Mark Twain, who said, "Twenty years from now you will be more disappointed by the things you didn't do than by the ones you did do. So throw off the bowlines. Sail away from the safe harbor. Catch the trade winds in your sails. Explore. Dream. Discover."

A study published in the October 2014 issue of the journal *Neuron* suggests that the brain's chemistry changes when we become curious. In essence, curiosity helps us to learn better and retain information longer. According to this study, when we are curious, our brain releases dopamine, similar to when we are rewarded with money or candy. Our brain, therefore, rewards us for being curious.

You, Kian, are a curious young boy. You don't need Mark Twain or a study to know that curiosity is rewarding in and of itself.

You are an inquisitive investigator, a tireless explorer, a creative problem solver. You are curious about everything you encounter. You will turn a light switch on and off over and over again, and in the process, learn more about cause and effect. You will pour water into any number of differently shaped containers (and inevitably on the ground and your clothes!), and in the process, learn about mass and volume. You use your mouth to discover different tastes and textures: the sweetness of a cookie, the bitterness of a lemon, and the icy feel of a popsicle. You find countless things to take apart and reassemble only to move quickly to the next challenge. Like most children, you have an innate desire to explore and learn by seeking out new experiences, interactions, settings, sounds, sights, and sensations.

I write these letters to share with you the many things I am learning from you. I endeavor to share the countless gifts you are giving me. But at the heart, at the core, of all of these lessons is this driving force you have to seek out new things: your curiosity.

I've spent much of my life fretting that I was boring and uninteresting. As an octogenarian, I am learning so many new things, though. First and foremost is the idea that being curious is what makes a person interested and interesting.

Kian, what an immeasurable gift it has been to observe your continuous example of nonstop curiosity. Curiosity has been a powerful companion in your toddler days. But it will also offer you great promise for the rest of your life. I hope you'll humor me as I share a few of my most important discoveries about some of the ways that curiosity impacts our lives.

Curiosity is essential to success. Curiosity propels you to challenge the status quo. It demands that you pay attention to how things are done and lead you to ask a lot of questions. As a toddler, one of your favorite questions appears to be "Why?" As an adult, I hope it continues to be a favorite!

Your thirst for knowledge impresses and inspires me. Somehow, you already seem to know that the path to both success and fulfillment is through inquiry. Unfortunately, I never got that message as a young person.

In junior high, I had a wonderful coach who was the principal at Compton High School. But Ed Moore was not just a great coach, he was an even better person. Later in life, as I was developing a Life Skills program for athletes, he suggested I become acquainted with Bloom's Taxonomy. This well-known diagram divides the way we learn into three domains, one of which is the *cognitive* domain. This domain emphasizes intellectual outcomes, but then further divides into categories arranged progressively from the lowest level of thinking—*simple recall*—to higher levels of thinking, such as *evaluation of information*, and eventually, *creation of original work*. It took me at least thirty years to fully understand the value of those distinctions. But I finally got the message put forth by Albert Einstein, who said "The important thing is not to stop questioning… Never lose a holy curiosity." An entire lifetime, Kian. That's how long it took me to understand the importance of being thoughtful and reflective when making life's decisions.

Curiosity checks our urge to react with defensiveness and ego. Quite simply, it's hard to be hostile and curious at the same time. In your life, you will engage in conversations for a multitude of purposes: to negotiate, to seek information, to reach understanding, to seek forgiveness. In those interactions, should the other person express resistance or hostility, try first to respond with curiosity and openness. In that way, you can move away from personalities and ideology and toward understanding and empathy.

Curiosity broadens perspective and creative thinking, which then leads to more solutions and opportunities. Curiosity drives creativity. It brings together multiple ideas and solutions. By being curious, you will be able to see new worlds and possibilities that are normally not visible. You will be able to detect things that are hidden behind the surface of normal life. It takes a curious person to look beyond the obvious and the easy to discover these new ideas and possibilities.

Curiosity promises excitement. The lives of curious people are far from boring. Curious people are neither dull nor routine, nor are they satisfied with a life that is without change. There are always new things that attract a curious person's interest and attention. There are always new "toys" to play with and explore.

My hope is that you, Kian, retain this immense curiosity you now have. Throughout all the years of your life, I hope you seek the new and different and that you surround yourself with people who do the same.

You've led me to a sharpening of my curiosity. Your inquisitiveness and example of asking questions has moved me toward a better version of myself in two ways. First, you have encouraged me to embrace an "I can" attitude even at my tender age (smile!). Simultaneously, you've helped me progress toward an "I enjoy" feeling.

Looking back on my life, the only time I recall having an "I can" attitude was as an athlete. I now realize my anxiety and self-doubt robbed me of taking advantage of my educational opportunities at Stanford, Princeton, and USC. If I had been more curious, I would have wrestled with the tough issues confronting society and me, personally. I would have asked big-picture questions and been an eager student who devoured insights and lessons. I also would have genuinely and enthusiastically involved myself in everything that was going on around me. I might have wondered why things worked the way they did and whether those things could be improved upon.

Instead, I let my anxiety guide me to find a stable job and write my term papers before the end of the first week of lectures. I succumbed to reading the course materials word for word. I tried to find the "right" answers. When it came to life's decisions, I was no better. I'm afraid I was persistently, stubbornly shallow and lacked insight or good judgement.

Now, though, you inspire me to move toward not only an "I *can*" attitude, but also toward an "I *enjoy*" feeling. I'm learning to go deeper in my thinking. I am challenged to venture toward solving my own problems and to manage my mental and health challenges. I now take more seriously my responsibility for my lifelong learning instead of looking for someone else to come up with the answers on my behalf. Most of all, I have found the courage to actively sense the world around me and engage in it, not just let it pass by. I am learning to see and to question the wonders of nature, the changing of seasons, the life cycle of a butterfly, the physics of a bird in flight, the passing of day into night.

Wonderment, curiosity, a sense of awe: these are the lessons I take from watching you explore your world. And these are the prerequisites of a more fulfilling life.

Much love,

Papa

CHAPTER FOUR
The Gifts of Effort and Energy

November 2020

Dear Kian,

Recently, I've thought a lot about your long, action-packed days, and how from roughly five in the morning until seven in the evening, you buzz around from one interesting thing to the next. I marvel at the effort, energy, and enthusiasm you seem to have in endless supply. I admit to being slightly envious of the way you are always on the lookout for new sources of excitement, or for anything that appears fun, engaging, and interesting, or that offers you a chance to learn a new skill. In short, Kian, you are "all in"—always energized, always alert, always ready for the next adventure.

This has prompted me to scratch my head and wonder: Where does your energy come from? For such an itty-bitty body, you seem to have a vast supply!

Reflecting back on my own life, I have experienced all levels of success and failure. I have achieved excellence, faced mediocrity, suffered disappointment. In every case, energy was always a factor. Could it be that simple? Does success hinge on that single element: energy?

Einstein apparently thought so. His renowned equation, $E = mc2$, proved that energy is the catalyst for everything. Harness it, and your options are unlimited.

But what is energy, exactly? World-renowned psychologists Freud, Jung, and Skinner all expressed thoughts on the subject, calling it self-gratification, motivation, and need satisfaction, among other things. Whatever we label it, however, it all boils down to this: Energy is the impetus that makes each of us perform. In other words, energy is the emotional fuel that gets us moving.

To understand this better, we need to examine what's known as the centrality of effort.

Many years ago, a couple of old college friends invited me to join them for the annual Bay to Breakers 12k, one of the world's largest and oldest footraces held annually in San Francisco. The race featured world-class athletes in addition to costumed runners and regular-old fun-loving folks who were just out for a pleasant day of running or walking through the streets of San Francisco. I wasn't in nearly good enough shape to run twelve kilometers (about seven-and-a-half miles), but I was playing basketball three times each week, so I figured I should at least be able to finish. Mostly, though, I just very much wanted to be with my friends. I naively signed up.

When the race started, I managed to keep up with the group for a while, and I was not struggling too badly. But then, after a few miles, I started to tire and fall behind. However, I desperately didn't want to be the guy who couldn't keep up. So, as a seasoned old jock, I mustered up enough energy to stay with group for the rest of our run—barely.

What's the point of my story? Well, first, to illustrate the foolishness of signing up for a race for which you have not trained. But mostly, it is to show that we almost always have an untapped reservoir of energy available to us. We simply need the right combination of thoughts to evoke the proper emotions—the ones that will propel us—and inevitably, we'll find that we can tap into that reservoir.

This story, though, leads me back to my original question—the one that first formed as I was watching you play and play and play some more. Where does energy come from? It's true that we can actually create human energy or emotional fuel ourselves. Different from physical, or vital energy, this particular energy comes from our emotions. It creates in each of us a *feeling impulse* to move us toward our goals. We call this process *motivation*.

As I watch you day after day, Kian, you seem to be naturally energetic and enthusiastic about practically anything and everything that interests you. This includes walking through a pile of leaves, marveling at a pine cone, delighting in seeing your mom's smile, and, of course, constantly trying to master new skills. Plus, any invitation to do something—"Let's take a walk!" or "Would you like to play in the park?" or "How about we read a book?"—brings forth your boundless enthusiasm and energy. This is natural now, but as we age, it is harder to maintain. So, let's look at it more closely:

Where does this energy come from, this emotional fuel that both excites and moves us?

First, it comes from having a goal, an idea, or a vision. It may start with a dream, or a desire for something you really want. Eventually, it becomes a target, something you hope to achieve individually or as a group or an organization. One way of thinking about vision is that it is the ability to see the opportunity in a situation. When that opportunity is verbalized, either inwardly to yourself or outwardly to a group of people, it has the ability to generate enthusiasm. But the key is to keep your eye on the goal or the idea that first inspired you. When you can do that, you may find it becoming the source of your energy.

Second, opportunities and challenges ignite the pursuit of a goal which then becomes a passion. A passion for something creates an emotional impulse—human energy or motivation—that then becomes the fuel that drives you. It is this fuel that keeps you moving toward your goal. People who are passionate will seek ways to fulfill their dreams. They will often identify avenues that others cannot see. A strong passion will enable you to find a way to achieve your goal—*any* goal, because through passion, we find energy.

But even with a passion driving you, you need a plan. As Aristotle said, "The soul never thinks without an image." Passion can build energy and excitement. But without a plan, a road map that leads to your destination, that energy is likely to dissipate quickly. Or you may find that you are expending it needlessly, with no sense of fulfillment or satisfaction.

Finally, I think it's important to highlight the significant connection between effort and enjoyment. As I've written in an earlier letter to you, my athletic and life experiences have been dominated by an exclusive focus on performance and its partner in crime: fear of failure. Enjoyment was not among my list of desired outcomes or goals.

Watching you and clearly witnessing the total fusion of your effort and enjoyment has dynamically altered my thinking. It is also challenging my behavior. Mihaly Csikszentmihalyi, in his book

Flow: The Psychology of Optimal Experience, notes how our feelings about an experience can mature over time. "Closing a contested business deal, or any piece of work well done, is enjoyable," he says. "None of these experiences may be particularly pleasurable at the time they are taking place, but afterward we think back on them and say, 'That was really fun' and wish they would happen again."

I have so many memories of game days as a young athlete. But I didn't realize the specialness of those experiences when they were happening. In fact, it's really hard to grasp now that effort and enjoyment aren't incompatible. I missed many opportunities to find pleasure in the hard work and shared efforts I was expending with teammates.

Kian, I want to end with a final thought about effort that our relationship has taught me. Effort is intimately connected to the development of friendship. There is something priceless about fusing your effort with someone else's that goes beyond the conventional meaning of fun. How I regret the dynamic duo of self-doubt and anxiety that made me the "serious guy" who failed to take time out from studying and college jobs to have a beer and hang out with teammates and classmates.

Choosing where we expend effort, then, is really about meaning. John Gardner has suggested that meaning is not something one stumbles across in life. We build meaning into our lives by the commitments we make. Lasting friendships are often forged in the crucible of shared commitment and struggle. In other words, through effort, we find meaning. Through meaning, we find what matters to us most in this life.

Once again, thank you, Kian, for your inspiration and leadership!

Papa

CHAPTER FIVE
The Gift of Learning How to Learn

December 2020

Greetings Kian,

Oscar Wilde, a flamboyant Irish poet in the 1800s well-known for his biting wit, once said, "Life is far too important a thing to ever talk seriously about." Not advice that a psychologist would find particularly amusing or useful!

Through these letters, I have struggled to express my deep appreciation for the inspiration and joy your young life has given me during what is undeniably a difficult time in my life. I have also begun to understand that these letters are what Wilde mockingly cautioned against: a talk with you about life.

First, we talked about the gift of connection you provided me. In subsequent letters, I've discussed the value of play and curiosity, as well as pondered the source of your boundless energy. In each letter, I find that I am gaining a deeper understanding of what motivates us as children and adults. I have new insights into my own life. And I am increasingly awed by the endless life lessons you seem to be providing me.

Today, I wish to talk about a phenomenon that I witness daily as I watch you play and connect and explore. It seems to be an intrinsic mission for you that I hope will transform into a lifetime mission: learning.

From the moment you were born, you quickly, efficiently, and automatically began to learn. By exploring your world as your growing body allowed, you tested out the unknown by using all of your senses. You imagined how the objects you encountered could be used in a multitude of ways. You continue to add knowledge and information to every corner of your brain, stashing it away like a squirrel preparing for winter. Your learning is not bound by textbooks or YouTube videos or lectures, however. You learn by seeing, hearing, feeling, doing, trying, failing, figuring it out, and getting it right.

For example, in just the first twenty-three months of your life, you've learned physical coordination. Through no (or little) instruction, you've figured out how to play, walk, talk, and eat. You've mastered some basic social skills and can now interact with your mom and dad and other family members, and negotiate with playmates at your preschool. You've gained the ability to communicate, think, problem-solve, react to others' emotions, and win over a stranger with a smile. In essence, you've discovered a great many things about our world by actively interacting with everything and everyone in it.

As I write to you today, knowing that you are likely reading this many years later, I worry about our current public school system. The educational process in the United States, with too few exceptions, has long abandoned the "learning by doing" philosophy that has served you so well in the early years of your life. Educators and those who wield power in the massive bureaucracy of public education seem to cling to this mistaken and even dangerous notion that young people learn just by watching and listening to others talk. Quite simply, that is not how our brains develop. We are experiential beings. As anyone watching you for a handful of minutes would attest, learning *is* experience.

John Dewey, American philosopher and educator, wisely noted that we all learn most effectively through experimentation and practice. I interpret this to mean that we learn best by doing the exact thing we are trying to learn, through direct experience with the world. Ask any lawyer, and they'll tell you that they learned more about law when they took their first case than they ever did in law school. A French teacher has no doubt discovered through years of grading verb conjugations that to truly learn a language, one must immerse themselves *in* that language.

Kian, in one of my previous letters, I mentioned that I had failed to take advantage of my educational experiences. I had the benefit of twelve years of college at some top-notch schools. I have four degrees, including a PhD. But like you, I've found that I've learned much more in the vast and wondrous classroom of life.

When I was a young kid in the 1930s, a teen in the 1940s, and a young adult in the 1950s, education was about imparting and receiving information. We went to school. We opened our textbooks and notebooks. Teachers spewed forth knowledge. We copied it, repeated it, and memorized it. Then, we demonstrated our mastery of it by feeding it back to them on tests or when questioned directly in class. In this system, I did very well.

I know now, however, that I was missing a key ingredient: ownership. Neither the system, nor the teacher, encouraged me (or even suggested that I try) to be the captain of my own learning. Nowhere was I allowed to explore as you do, to try and fail as you do, to use the world as the classroom and naturally seek out the lessons I wanted to take from it. In school and in sports, I was guided to learn what someone else had determined was important. I realize now that my mind and my heart should have guided my educational path. I should have had more stake in this lifelong journey to learn, grow, and become the best version of myself.

Kian, I guess what I'm trying to say is this: All real learning is self-learning. Until you apply what you learn to your own experience, it really isn't learning at all.

My fervent wish for you is that you adopt this simple learning strategy that I failed to find for most of my life. Take charge of your learning, Kian. Own it. Be responsible for it. Let it be driven by your passions and curiosities. Let it have meaning and depth. And let all your knowledge and insight connect you to this wondrously amazing classroom that is full of endless things to explore: life. It sounds so easy. And in some ways, it is. But let's talk about this effective learning strategy I've shared and how to utilize it best.

First, understand that metacognition plays a key role in our learning. This is a concept that I wish had informed my youth. Metacognition, an awareness of our own thinking, challenges us to examine the way we think. Sometimes, perhaps often, we are unaware of our own thought processes. In other words, we don't actually know what we are thinking as we are thinking it. Countless times in my life, I would have been better served (and I would have better served those around me), if I'd stopped to ask myself, "George, why are you solving your problem in this manner?" Too often, I simply forged ahead without knowing the reasons behind my thoughts.

Second, recognize that the best learning is self-directed. We've all experienced a desire to learn, a "fire in the belly" moment, an internal excitement to explore something new. And it's almost never in an attempt to memorize something for a test or quiz. No, our interest is piqued when we come across something—a topic, a skill, a puzzle—that connects to our lives somehow or creates a feeling of excitement, passion, or curiosity. Research indicates that such intrinsic motivation (doing something because it is inherently interesting or enjoyable) unsurprisingly leads to higher quality learning.

Third, don't overlook the importance of practice. Learning how to learn is a skill, and just like we learn any skill, deliberate practice is essential. I discovered in my athletic experience that the only way to truly acquire a skill is to overlearn it. Repetition is the key. To really learn something, one must practice that newly acquired skill beyond the point of initial mastery.

Put another way, learning how to learn takes time. There is no shortcut. The path to a more effective approach to learning requires that you possess a capacity and desire to discover, plan and set aside time to evaluate your progress, and adopt a fresh strategy toward the endeavor.

Finally, embrace the idea that learning is all about experimenting. We learn through trial and error. Mohandas K. Gandhi, who titled his autobiography *The Story of My Experiments with Truth,* calls our attention to an atmosphere of experimental risk-taking. This mindset prescribes that we take one small step at a time, but expect to experience some temporary regression. With each small success, we breed more success, and adopt a willingness to persevere. Ultimately, we arrive at a more substantial new strategy for how we learn.

As I have ended every letter, I will end this one with gratitude. This journey has been one of learning and exploration, one that has trumped the many years I spent in classrooms. Thank you, Kian, for inspiring me to take it.

With love,

Papa

CHAPTER SIX
The Gift of Positivity

December 2020

Dear Kian,

You have an almost nonstop smile. Your joyful spirit and frequent happy dances throughout these first two years of your life, in turn, never fail to make *me* to smile. Many mornings, I felt I could have sat and watched you all day; it was that wonderful. Now that you are older, I'm sure you've had some difficult challenges since then. At whatever age you are now, it is almost assured that you have faced sadness, defeat, and setbacks. Yet I suspect that your smile and positive thinking are still your steadfast companions.

In significant ways, I was unlike you as a boy. I don't remember feeling the kind of positivity I see in you. Instead, I was an anxious guy. I never learned to play unless it was on a basketball court. Relaxing was a foreign concept. I can't remember many times that I stopped to impulsively enjoy time with friends, grab a beer, or just hang out with them.

Once again, Kian, I am indebted to your leadership and the inspiration you continually provide. It has led me to revisit, or—perhaps more accurately—motivate, me to take a longer and deeper look at an old question that has befuddled me throughout my life. It is an oft-asked question, but one worth examining: What role does positive thinking play in our behavior and success?

As I write this letter, you are a toddler. Your language skills are increasing every day, if not every hour. Though you don't always have the words, you are asking more and more questions: "What is this?" and "What are you doing?" and "How does that work?" You want to know the what, how, and why of things. All open and good questions! And each one is an avenue to learning and growing.

I, too, wrestle with my own questions. As my

questions about positivity swirl in my brain, I can imagine your tilted head as you ask me, as you so often do, "Papa, why are you doing that?" At two, you already understand the importance of metacognition!

Ben Hogan, one of the greatest professional golfers in history, may help us begin our exploration of positivity and positive thinking. One of his famous saying is, "Golf is twenty percent technique and eighty percent mental." Similar to golf, our attitudes and beliefs influence the way we experience life. If we think negatively, we ultimately fail. But if we think positively? We surely succeed. As Henry Ford once proclaimed, "Whether you believe you can do a thing or not, you are right." What you believe, you become.

And yet, if it is so simple, then why are there so many books written on the subject? If it is as easy as waking up and thinking the day will be great, then why do so many people struggle with anxiety and depression?

Because, of course, it is *not* simple.

In my last letter, I talked about the idea of practice being instrumental to learning to learn more effectively. Practicing positive thinking is also key. But to truly be a positive thinker, there are some other things worth considering.

First, flexibility is important. In her book *Mindset: The New Psychology of Success*, Carol S. Dweck describes two different ways of thinking. The first is a fixed mindset. This type obscures the unlimited boundaries of our potential. Success is about proving how smart or talented one is. It's about validating oneself. Failure is a setback, and something to avoid. It equates to not fulfilling one's potential. Getting a bad grade, losing a ball game, or getting fired all signify a lack of something important in one's life—ability, intelligence, talent, likability. In short, failure is falling short of one's potential.

A growth mindset, however, involves a thought process of self-belief and affirmation. You believe in yourself. You adhere to the idea that effort is what makes you smart or talented. You know you have to stretch a little to learn something new, and it might be uncomfortable, and you might not even get it right the first try. But in the process, you are developing, learning, growing.

Dweck makes it clear that mindsets are just beliefs. So, it's a choice; we can choose to have either a fixed or growth mindset. Because they are beliefs, controlled by us within our own minds, we can also change them.

Second, positive thinking can create change. In his book *The Inner Game of Tennis: The Classic Guide to the Mental Side of Peak Performance*, Timothy Gallwey states, "I know of no single factor that more greatly affects our ability to perform than the image we have of ourselves." William James, the great American philosopher, made the same point when he said, "Human beings, by changing the inner belief of their minds, can change the outer aspects of their lives."

So, how do we improve our inner beliefs and reclaim our innate potential? There are many possible ways of looking at this challenge, but I like to consider what is standing in our way. A big part of positive thinking is having a positive self-image. Personally, my self-image has always been limited. It improved when I played sports, but was much lower as a student, husband, psychologist, consultant, and writer. Clearly (and I'm working on it), I must achieve a greater regard for myself.

Fear of failure is another roadblock for many of us, myself included. While it has admittedly been a great motivator that has brought me abundant recognition throughout my life, it was often the total focus of that day's activity or game. Fear of failure, and my preoccupation with it, ultimately led to a total disregard for the enjoyment and fun of the experience.

Though these letters have been somewhat of a self-awakening and a way to reflect on the missteps of my life, I realize I also need to curb my habit of self-criticism, which I fear has been all too evident in them. Kian, if you had my same tendency toward self-criticism, you might have never learned to walk or talk. Fortunately for you, you are inherently free of self-criticism at your current age. Fortunately for me, I'm learning to accept my mistakes even as I write to you.

In my quest to embrace positivity, I will conclude with some ideas that have grown out of observing you. Determined to tackle positive thinking in my own mindset, this is a bit of a daily checklist for me, but maybe you'll find some benefit in it as well.

1. Smile often. Yours is the most beautiful smile on the planet. For first two years of your life, your smile has brought joy to others. Smiling makes us feel better, but it also makes those around us feel better.

2. Maintain good posture. It is an old-fashioned notion. But standing up straight, chest out, stomach in, and shoulders back is a great habit. Holding yourself in this way sends a signal to your brain to feel more confident. I don't know how much I'll be able to accomplish this at eighty-six, but I know it will lift my spirits to make the effort.

3. Avoid clock-watching. I know how fascinating clocks are to you, especially Nana's cuckoo clock. For you, clocks are about fun and curiosity. For me, clocks remind me that time is going by too fast. Avoid wishing for the time to pass. It will. Try to enjoy those minutes instead.

4. Consider taking baths, not showers. Baths provide more time to relax and reflect. When we have a few unhurried and calm moments to ourselves, we are more prone to a positive mindset.

5. Greet others with a hearty hello. Your enthusiasm is a gift; share it with others. The more we attempt to lift up others, the better we will all be.

6. Concentrate on something positive from your day before you go to sleep. Make your last conscious thought of the day a joyous one. Your dreams will be more pleasant, and you will awaken more refreshed.

Changing your mindset, like so many tasks in life, is not easy. It requires motivation and desire, practice and dedication. But in the wise words of George Bernard Shaw: "Progress is impossible without change, and those who cannot change their minds cannot change anything."

As always, I end with gratitude to you, Kian, for helping me change my mindset and see the beauty in feeling good about myself and the world around me.

With love,

Papa

CHAPTER SEVEN
The Gift of Leadership

December 2020

Dear Kian,

I can imagine your puzzlement, possibly even laughter, as you read my previous letters and see my repeated thanks for the inspiration and leadership you have provided me. I can almost hear you now, saying, "Oh, come on, Papa, leadership? I wasn't even two years old!"

The truth is that right now you already have so many qualities of a natural leader, grabbing my attention and being assertive in simple and wonderful ways. You seem to understand, as I awkwardly try to lower myself to the floor to play with you, that in this moment, I need you to "lead." And you respond eagerly, bringing me a toy, a book, a spinner, or a truck to further our playtime. You lead in other ways, as well, by welcoming me and others with the world's greatest smile (I may be a bit impartial), or by bursting into a happy dance. You know exactly how to entice me to play with you. Your excitement is the encouragement I need to take a walk, venture outside, play a game—seemingly small moments, but ones that always make an enormous difference in my outlook, attitude, and overall health.

Before you were born but in the later years of my professional life, I designed and administered a youth leadership development program called *Lead2Play*! Through my experiences and research, I've come to believe that true leadership has less to do with a *position* and more to do with a *disposition*. Leadership is how we view life and people, how we leverage our strengths and influence on others. It doesn't require power, seniority, or position. I would argue, in fact, that leadership supersedes one's status or position. Everyone, in every facet of life and at every age, has the power to lead. The program that I developed seeks to encourage and foster that view in young people by providing experiences that give them opportunities to practice and develop the skills and mindset of true leadership.

In this moment, as I write this letter, we face innumerable problems as a society, a nation, and a world. We are in the middle of a pandemic. Our nation is sharply divided politically and ideologically. We face a global climate that is changing and threatening to impact us in ways seen and unseen. If we rely only on the positioned leaders—those who serve as heads of governments and organizations—to solve them, I fear we face a losing battle. It's an insurmountable challenge. Instead, every single human alive right now has an obligation to lead, take ownership of these challenges, and leverage our own strengths, abilities, and social capital to move us toward solutions. Indeed, we need our young people to lead now more than ever. In fact, I firmly believe that we must enlist young people in the cause of leadership and help them understand its value and its impact.

Through *Lead2Play!*, I hoped to share the idea that real leaders practice two fundamental duties: 1) They solve problems; 2) They serve people.

When we see leadership as having these two primary functions, it becomes a catalyst to viewing leadership a bit differently.

First, we view leadership as an action we take, rather than the position we hold. In other words, when we move away from an emphasis on the noun *leader*, we move toward an emphasis on the verb *to lead*. Leadership is much less about climbing a power structure or establishing one's place in a hierarchy. It's about doing things that impact people.

Next, we begin to understand that leadership is about taking personal and social responsibility to work together to serve others. Through *Lead2Play!*, young leaders were fostered to lead peers and younger children in areas of play, physical activity, and sports. Everyone has the opportunity to lead. While not everyone can lead in every situation, everyone does have the capacity to step up, take responsibility, and work with others on shared goals.

Kian, perhaps you are wondering: Where is Papa going with all this stuff about leadership? Good question.

I want to introduce (or maybe reinforce) the concept of self-leadership to you. In so many ways, leadership is about taking charge of your life. It encompasses how you lead your own life, set your own course, follow it, and correct it as you go. Two thousand years ago, a great teacher named Hillel wrote a little poem that would rhyme if it were written Aramaic:

> *If I am not for myself, then who will be for me?*
>
> *But if I am only for myself, then what am I?*
>
> *And if not now, when?*

There are two powerful messages within this poem. The first is that in every age, people have had to struggle to be themselves. From the beginning of time, we have tried to face challenges and solve problems on our own by relying on our own decisions, running our own shows, taking charge of our own lives. I don't know if there is comfort or consternation in this first message, but the fact remains: Humans are naturally inclined to second-guess themselves, it seems.

The second message lies in the words, "if only for myself, what am I?" The late John W. Gardner, former Secretary of Health, Education and Welfare, a man ahead of his time, said that one of his chief concerns about our educational system was that it unwittingly injected students with an "anti-leadership vaccine." Sadly, our educational institutions continue this practice by conditioning students to blend in and go with the flow. The system is designed to indoctrinate today's youth to never question the status quo. Instead, our schools should be inspiring youth leaders to bring about change. Students should be encouraged and taught to question and challenge current practices and seek to find better ones.

Hopefully, your world and our country are in better shape now than when I wrote these words. Still, I have no doubt that on the day you read this, as on the day I write it, the need for effective leaders at every level of society—in our families, at work, in our communities, throughout our nation—is desperately needed. Leaders who can help us overcome the limitations of our own selfishness, weaknesses, and fears. Leaders who can motivate us to work harder, do better, and instigate change in every aspect of our lives. Leaders who know that the power of a collaborative community achieves far more than we can get ever get done on our own.

Kian, before we go any farther, I want to make sure you understand that I am not talking about a future job or career. Indeed, I changed my major in college as well as my career enough times to be embarrassed. I'm challenging you to shift your sense of identity, to see leadership as identifying your gifts and using them to serve others, and not as a title or position you might hold. I want you to see leadership as leveraging your influence through solving problems and serving people.

As I've said earlier, right now, you are a natural leader. You are curious and always on the hunt to improve your day. You are willing to learn about things that are new to you, even if they are hard or make you uncomfortable. You are a problem-solver who likes to fix things that need fixing (and some that don't!). You don't let failure stop you from finding new and creative solutions. You also challenge *me* to be my best, to learn and grow, to consider what is possible, to step up, and to ultimately get it done. Your daycare center's daily reports suggest your popularity with your fellow toddlers, and that they look to you for answers. You do all this naturally.

It is my fervent hope that you will embrace your natural gifts for leadership and further their development. Leadership, however, can be a daunting prospect. In thinking of your role as a leader, I would encourage you to spend some time considering your responses to these questions:

Do you want to serve others? How?

Do you want to impact others? In what ways?

Do you want to improve some aspect of society? If so, what is a good first step?

A few findings over the years have helped me understand leadership better. The first is that most leaders have a vision, an idea of "what can be." A vision is a blueprint of a preferred tomorrow. It can help us see in our imagination what is not yet visible in reality. J. Oswald Sanders, Christian author and speaker, believed that leadership is synonymous with influence. It's not about titles or positions. It's about bringing your influence to the people in your life: classmates, teammates, or coworkers. But leadership is rarely comfortable. Why? It often requires a person to take a risk. Leaders take initiative when there is not a guarantee of success. They are willing to move forward knowing that nobody may follow. Finally, true leaders understand the importance of having a sense of ownership regarding their mission. Leaders who make excuses or who blame someone else when something goes wrong are missing one of the fundamental traits of leadership. Real leaders ascribe to the team philosophy of "All for one and one for all."

Kian, this country and this world need leaders. Ones who understand the value of a broad and genuine smile, ones who are willing to bring the toy to a weary but willing grandfather, ones who are naturally encouraging and strive to operate at their best.

Thank you, Kian, for inspiring me to write these thoughts and for reminding me that there are leaders like you in this world.

Love,

Papa

CHAPTER EIGHT
The Gift of Making Mistakes

December 2020

Dear Kian,

I've already told you how much I enjoy watching you try new things. Every day, you learn something new. Climbing up and sitting in big chairs. Balancing while clambering up and down a steep hill. Walking backwards. Using words to make yourself understood. Making new friends. Equally important, though sometimes terrifying for those tasked with watching you, is letting you make mistakes.

Marty Miller, a former college professor at Iowa State University, loved working with young people and coaching them in softball. While it has been many years since our paths have crossed, I fondly remember Marty's core belief that the practice field and baseball diamond were "Centers of Mistakes." He adamantly believed that these were safe spaces where you didn't worry about "goofing up." To introduce his point, Marty annually wore a special T-shirt on the first day of his team's softball practice. The motto on the front read, "MISTAKES R WONDERFUL OPPORTUNITIES 2 LEARN!" His shirt captured so well a major premise of his coaching approach: the "mistakes center" concept, which illustrates that the best way to teach skills and establish a fun environment at the same time is to encourage players to take risks and try new things.

Marty knew that mistakes are the lifeblood of learning. Without the willingness to make mistakes and learn from them, we get stuck, and all our learning shrivels up. Kian, I continue to be impressed with how much you are learning and soaking up about the world around you. But you do, of course, experience failure.

The remarkable thing is that those failures don't seem to discourage you. When you were learning to walk, you would fall down and get back up before any adult could even react. When you try to feed your-self and miss your mouth, it's simple: you try again. A square block that won't fit in a circular hole? No problem—you just keep trying until you find the aptly shaped hole.

For you, as a toddler, making a mistake carries no stigma, shame, or embarrassment. As we pass through adolescence, middle age, and into our later years, we tend to want to avoid mistakes at all costs. They challenge many positive illusions we may have about ourselves. Unfortunately, this thinking starts to slow down our ability to learn. It is precisely our willing-ness to experiment and to accept the numerous trials and errors that follow that drives the learning process.

In my other letters, I talked about the impor-tance of relationships. I remember a popular slogan: "No pain, no gain." Four words that serve as a mo-tivating mantra for many people in the sports world. Yet, in other facets of our lives, we reflexively avoid pain, dodge adversity, and run away from uncertainty. I watched recently, and somewhat nervously, as you prepared to stretch the bounds of your universe by climbing to the top of the play structure at the local park a few blocks from your home. You stood right under that jungle gym, looked up at it in awe, and per-haps said to yourself in a voice I imagine was filled with enthusiasm and a bit of fear: "Today's the day. I'm going to give it a go!" For you, that play structure represented an important test of childhood. You are likely not aware of the pain that could result if you fell off of it. (Though every adult in your life is acutely aware of it, to be sure!)

It is part of human nature to avoid pain. But pain, adversity, uncertainty, and failure, despite the hardships they bring, are where we truly experience life. Through these experiences, we can learn so many things about ourselves, the world, and what is possible.

For one, we learn about personal responsibility. As we move through adolescence, young adulthood, and finally adulthood, the relationship between what we do and what happens to us is ever-present. This awareness is quite different from earlier years in childhood, where we were offered protections and warnings before we set off to do something that might have dire consequences. In this gradual way, we learn to take ownership of our actions, and when we do something unwise—stay out too late, spend too much money, avoid doing the laundry for three weeks—there are consequences.

Mistakes also help us learn coping skills. Life is a journey filled with occasions of joy and happiness interspersed with frustrations, rejections, and conflict. How we navigate these tough times defines who we really are. Learning the skills that can help us cope is critically important. Such skills include a positive attitude, reaching out to friends, looking for creative solutions to problems, and getting enough sleep and exercise.

Two of the biggest things that mistakes teach us are perseverance and resilience. One of the world's greatest inventors, Thomas Edison, was also one of the greatest failures of his generation. He tested various materials for the filament of the electric light bulb and was wrong more than 6,000 times. One of Edison's greatest attributes, however, was his relentless persistence. "I have not failed. I've just found 10,000 ways that won't work," he remarked. Some of the greatest things in this lifetime are achieved when we fail first.

Which leads me to the final lesson that mistakes can teach us: how to overcome failure. Kian, watching you learn to walk was stressful for me. Your initial steps included several falls. I worried, as you neared sharp and potentially damaging corners that seemed to be everywhere you turned, that a fall might result in a bump or bruise, or worse. A few of your falls were painful for you and hard for me to watch. But you persisted until you learned from your repeated failures to master one of the most difficult and challenging of athletic skills: walking. While none of your falls were indicative of major setbacks, we all encounter obstacles and become acquainted with the agony of defeat as we move through our lives. Those who can move past that defeat will likely find both success and fulfillment.

Kian, I have stumbled, fallen, and ultimately survived my share of setbacks over the years. Through these failures, I have learned that before I decide to quit something I have endeavored to do, I ask myself these questions:

> ***Why did I pursue this in the first place?***
> Every decision or endeavor we undertake will have its challenges and setbacks. When things get difficult or dire, it is easy to ignore why we made our choice originally. But if it was worth choosing to do, it is likely worth choosing to see it through to the end.

Why do I feel the need to quit? We often want to quit something when it makes us unhappy or uncomfortable. In addition to understanding why we made our decision in the first place, figuring out why we are thinking of giving up makes it easier to decide what's driving the decision to quit.

Have I done everything I can to make this work for me? Often, we quit too easily, before we have exhausted all of our options. Sometimes, we can ask for help or simply go about what we are trying to do in a different way.

And, lastly, what do I gain by quitting? Everything we do has a cost, whether we choose to do it or not. Making either a mental or a physical list of the benefits and drawbacks of quitting can help us know if we are making the right decision.

This is much easier said than done, but one thing I have learned in my lifetime is to face my fears instead of letting them fuel my decisions. I like how Shakespeare put it in *Measure for Measure*:

"Our doubts are traitors,

and make us lose the good we oft might win

by fearing to attempt."

Kian, as I've mentioned previously, self-doubt has been a constant companion of mine. My wish for you is that you learn how to face your fears and make your decisions without listening to a nagging self-doubt. Instead, go forth with as much grace and self-assuredness as possible.

I have spoken sometimes regretfully of my time playing sports; I have felt I let my desire to win usurp the joy of playing. But playing sports taught me many things. One of them was this, a quote by Earl Nightingale: "Never give up on a dream just because of the time it will take to accomplish it. The time will pass anyway."

It's important to remember that failure is a distinguishing attribute for many of the most respected men and women in history. History books write of Abraham Lincoln as a fearless leader, a bold unifier, a wise statesman. But Lincoln lost numerous times in his life.

- He failed in business at age twenty-two.

- He was defeated for the state legislature at the age of twenty-three.

- He suffered a nervous breakdown at the age of twenty-seven.

- He was defeated for speaker at the age of twenty-nine.

- He was defeated for congressional nomination at the age of thirty-four.

- He was defeated for the Senate at the age of forty-six.

- He was defeated for the vice president of the United States at the age of forty-seven.

- He was defeated again for the Senate at the age of forty-nine.

Yet Abraham Lincoln never quit. He was elected president of the United States at the age of fifty-one. With each fall, he rose again, and eventually he reached his destination, gaining the respect and admiration of the nation and people. We can all learn from his perseverance.

Kian, as I close this letter, may I give you a final word of encouragement? Continue as you did in your childhood. Never stop seeing the possibilities and potential that others may fail to look for. Learn how to handle your anxiety and doubts so you are free to see new and challenging things. Have the courage to use the strength and creativity you most certainly possess. This openness to opportunities and possibilities that others may or may not see is your answer to any mistakes or failures that you may experience.

Author Neil Gaiman wrote this about mistakes:

"Make glorious, amazing mistakes. Make mistakes nobody's ever made before. Don't freeze, don't stop, don't worry that it isn't good enough, or it isn't perfect, whatever it is: art, or love, or work or family or life. Whatever it is you're scared of doing, do it. Make your mistakes, next year and forever."

Make your mistakes, Kian, now and forever.

With gratitude,

Your Papa

CHAPTER NINE
The Gift of Friendship

December 2020

Dear Kian,

We often think of friendship as that relationship between two peers who enjoy each other's company, share common likes, and have built a trusted bond. But friendship is really quite simply a mutual affection between two people.

Today, I want to thank you for the wonderful friendship that we are developing. It is one that bolsters my spirits while providing depth, enjoyment, and so many moments of fun. How, you are undoubtedly asking with some measure of skepticism, could we have formed a friendship with you not yet two years old? I would begin my response by saying this: As a toddler, you possessed a visible desire to belong, to be accepted. You wanted the attention of those around you, and to be viewed as having valuable contributions to make. I was simply one among a growing number of people in your world—family members, daycare teachers, and playmates—who benefitted from your mission to seize every opportunity to learn new skills and make new friends.

Even as you foster new friendships nearly daily, however, remember that true friendship is rare, especially in today's world. To anyone paying attention, various forms of social media—Twitter, Facebook, LinkedIn, or any of the countless other modern-day virtual watercoolers—are changing the way we live. Indeed, with so many "followers," we might feel as if we are suddenly awash in friends. Yet in real time, we're changing the way we conduct relationships. Face-to-face chatting is giving way to texting and messaging; people even prefer these electronic exchanges to simply talking on a phone. We may have plenty of acquaintances, but these days it seems we have fewer close friends to whom we can turn and share our deepest concerns.

Recent studies have shown that there has been a significant decline in the number and quality of friendships formed in the United States. Friendships, therefore, are no longer something we should assume will just become part of our lives as we live and grow. Instead, they are relationships we need to actively seek out and foster with intentionality.

Maybe you have continued, as you did at age two, to build and maintain friendships with ease. I hope so. But like so many things in our lives, I don't think it ever hurts to spend some time in self-reflection, asking ourselves questions to "check-in" or gauge how well we are fulfilling our role as a friend to others. So, a few questions to facilitate that reflection:

Are relationships a top priority in your life? Oh, how I wish I had spent more time examining this question in my own life when I was a younger person. Instead, my priorities were always playing sports and achieving good grades during my school years, and then building a career and making a living after college and graduate school. Don't get me wrong: I was popular and well-liked, mostly because of my athletic success. I always seemed to know a lot of people. I had lots of acquaintances. But only now do I realize that genuine friendship occurs only when two ingredients are present: commitment and time. The greater the commitment and the more time spent together, the better the likelihood that you will develop deep and lasting friendships.

Do you cultivate transparency? The most important ingredient in any relationship is *who you are*. As Ralph Waldo Emerson, essayist and philosopher, put it, "Who you are speaks so loudly, I can't hear what you are saying." Research tells us that self-disclosure—not common interests—is the basis for all deep friendships. The only way to build lasting relationships is to let people see who we *really* are—flaws and all. Don't hide away those things that make you real and genuine from the people you care about.

Do you work to maintain relationships that are important to you? Many people falsely believe that once they become involved in a friendship, they no longer need to put any work into the relationship. It's as if a friendship will somehow magically sustain itself and continue on just as it was when it first started. The truth is that relationships— all of them, whether marriages, friendships, work relationships, or family—take effort. Furthermore, they can only deepen and strengthen when we build stepping stones of honest and open communication, where both people are willing to tread. Honesty and vulnerability must occur when two people are trying to get to know each other and build trust. Plus, when we admit how we are feeling about someone else's actions, behaviors, and words, and why we feel that way, we often open a window into our own self-awareness. Owning our reactions, recognizing that they are based on our past experiences, and then understanding the reasons behind those reactions can help free us up from old baggage. Self-awareness has a huge therapeutic value.

It is also helpful to remember that friendships are a risk. We are taking a chance on another person. But by being open, we give off positive energy in our interactions that in itself bodes well for building trust and optimism in these friendships. Starting a new relationship puts us in touch with our own feelings, enables better communication and understanding, and ultimately allows us to grow and develop as humans. Staying in and maintaining that relationship means working through the rough spots to find greater understanding on the other side of them.

Though I am still learning about myself, I have spent many years of my career trying to understand people. And while I won't claim to be the foremost expert, I believe I do have some insights I can share with you. I don't mean to lecture, Kian, but to offer what wisdom I have gleaned from my own life, in case you find it relevant to your own.

First, healthy relationships require both effort and compromise. It's quite possible that the most damaging pathology of our time is rigidity. So often, we tend to be unbending in our beliefs and opinions. However, when someone says something that challenges your beliefs, there is always a choice: to learn or defend. The first has the potential to broaden your perspectives and strengthen your relationship; the latter will nearly always lead to walls and distance.

Second, listening is still the most essential tool to building relationships. In fact, listening is one of the most important skills we can learn. There is no correlation between being right and being part of strong human relationships. It is self-defeating to hold firm to one's own hypotheses when it comes to other people. In short, if you have the courage to listen, your relationships will benefit.

Still, all relationships are stretched, challenged, and tested at some point. One thing to consider when that happens is that the problem is rarely the problem. It is usually only a *symptom* of something much deeper. It may require time and self-reflection to understand what that is. When it comes to conflict, it's also often wise to distinguish between "venting" and problem-solving. One feels good, but often does nothing to end the conflict. The other is uncomfortable, but has the potential to not just solve the problem at hand, but ultimately deepen the understanding between two people. In a previous letter, I spoke of a saying in sports, "No pain, no gain." To strengthen something, whether it's our muscles or our friendships, we must be willing to tolerate a little discomfort now and then.

Finally, the four dimensions of a healthy relationship are respect, empathy, concreteness, and genuineness. Relationships that are bound on all sides by these four things have less chance of "going off the rails." Respect means asking questions instead of making accusations. Empathy involves allowing the people you care about to make mistakes and learning from them—and hoping that they offer you the same opportunity. Concreteness means understanding the value of praise. It was the author Mark Twain who said, "I can live for two months on one good compliment." And genuineness means putting yourself out there even when it is terrifying, even when you risk rejection.

The bottom line is this, Kian. Friendships make life better. Your friendship has certainly added meaning and joy to my life.

With gratitude,

Papa

CHAPTER TEN
The Gift of Being Yourself

December 2020

Dear Kian,

I sit down to write this letter just a few days before Christmas. As 2020 comes to an end, I realize, with a

somewhat heavy heart, that I have just one more letter I'd like to compose. I have enjoyed writing these,
Kian—buoyed by both the connection I've felt with
you, and the insights I've gained about myself and
about life. I hope that you have found them enjoyable
to read, and perhaps you've even gleaned some new
insights as well.

I've started most of these letters by sharing an
observation, a reflection, or an example of gratitude.
Today, I'll take a different tack, a rather unusual one.
I'd like to give you a quick synopsis of *The Muppet
Movie*, which you first watched this week.

Released in 1979, the movie follows Kermit the
Frog as he embarks on a cross-country trip to Holly-
wood to audition for a part in a movie. Along the way,
he encounters several other Muppets, all of whom
share the same hope of finding success in professional
show business. He is also being pursued by Doc Hop-
per, an evil restaurateur who intends to enlist Kermit
as a spokesperson for his frog legs business.

As far as movies go, it's a pretty typical family movie with a straightforward plot and a feel-good
ending. But to you, it was magic.

Let me back up a bit. As we often did, your Nana
and I arrived at your house yesterday in the late af-
ternoon. Your parents both currently work from home
and usually finish up by about five in the evening.
On this day, like so many others, we came over to let
your dad get dinner started, to take you for a walk or
a drive, or just spend some time with you. I never fail
to look forward to this time with you.

But last night, when Nana and I arrived, you and your dad were glued to the television and *The Muppet Movie*. Your excitement and interest were obvious: you bounced up and down on the couch, smiled frequently at all of us, and squealed in delight at your on-screen "buddies" Kermit and Miss Piggy. Then, when the Muppets were captured and guns were drawn, your face contorted, and it was easy to see your anxiety and distress.

There was nothing inherently unusual about any of this. What child has not shown interest in a movie? But what struck me was your sensitivity and concern—your innate empathy for these fictional characters. As the director undoubtedly hoped, you were rooting for Kermit and his friends. But more than that, you seemed to understand their pain, their fear, and their triumph.

I have marveled often at your ever-developing thoughtfulness and sensitivity. I am reminded of a chapter in a book that I have not looked at in more than fifty years. Still, its message has obviously remained significant to me all these years later. The book, *On Becoming a Person: A Therapist's View of Psychotherapy*, is by Carl R. Rogers, who is widely regarded as one of the most eminent psychologists. In the chapter entitled, "This is Me," Dr. Rogers, instead of giving advice, encourages certain personal choices that he believes will move his readers toward being the people they would like to be.

In that spirit, I'd like to share some observations I've made as I've watched you. The manner in which you interact with and perceive your world is both fascinating and noteworthy. My hope is to inspire you, as Dr. Rogers inspired me, to reflect on your two-year-old self and perhaps gain a few insights that might help you strive to be the best version of yourself.

Let's start by examining and celebrating your "beginner's mind." Kian, I observe you doing what most might see as mundane tasks—choosing a book, picking up a leaf from the ground, pointing at something that's caught your eye. Each of those tasks—and in fact much of what you do—is novel for you. You look around wide-eyed, awed, curious, and ask a lot of questions. You soak up the sights, smells, and sounds of your environment. Everywhere you turn, you find something that intrigues you or prompts you to think, "Isn't that interesting?" instead of dismissing it as something you already know, or something that is dull, meaningless, and lackluster. This way of looking at the world as a new and wondrous place is natural for you right now. But what if we, as fully grown adults, took a page from your book? What if we chose to see our world as a place full of new discoveries? What if we adopted a "beginner's mind?" Think of the delight each day would bring!

Your ability to react to each situation in such a way is due, in part, to your wonderful authenticity. You are one hundred percent authentic all the time. To be "authentic" is literally to be your own "author," as the two words derive from the same Greek root. At age two, you are naturally programmed to discover your native energies and desires, and to find your own way of acting on them. When you do that, you are not attempting to live up to an image set by culture, family tradition, or some authority outside yourself. You are simply being *you*—with no pretenses, fake smiles, or guarded responses. What an amazing world this might be if we all managed to hold onto that authenticity throughout our entire lives. What if we all managed to be confident in who we are and embrace our inner selves?

Kian, I want to reiterate what a priceless experience it has been to witness your personal development and to see that your behavior comes from *inside* you. It is not dictated by what is "cool" or "popular." It is not molded by your desire to be accepted or lauded. It is, instead, a reflection of what's important to you, what you hope to accomplish in a moment, or how you are feeling.

Reflecting back now on my youth, I've come to certain realizations. I've spent a good many years embracing a mistaken belief that the way forward was forged by reaching *outside* myself and proving to *others* that I was worthy. Come to think of it, I'm convinced that my friends probably also believed that they had to prove themselves or perform in some way to be successful. As a psychologist once told me, we often become "human doings" before "human beings."

"Self-esteem" is an oft-used term, especially by teachers, parents, and psychologists. Building a child's self-esteem is something of utmost importance. But what is self-esteem? It's an individual's perception of their own worth. In other words, it is the relationship you have with yourself. However, it's often confused with self-image and self-concept. Self-image is the degree to which one believes they are liked or respected by others. Self-concept is an understanding of one's identity.

Understanding one's identity is an introspective process that requires that we be deeply honest, both with ourselves and others. Norman Lear, the former television writer and producer, deeply understood the process. He described self-actualization as something like this: "First and foremost, find out what it is you're about, and be that. Be what you are, and don't lose it.... It's very hard to be who we are, because it doesn't seem to be what anyone wants." But, as Lear demonstrated, it's the only way to truly fly.

Abraham Lincoln once said, "Give me six hours to chop down a tree and I will spend the first four sharpening my axe." President Lincoln understood something that too few of us buy into today—especially leaders—and even fewer people actually practice. It's the art of development: the vital importance of improvement and preparation. It's identifying ways that we can improve every day, and then committing to making those improvements as best we can.

The ability to do this, examine our own strengths and weaknesses, is a measure of our emotional intelligence, or EQ. EQ stands for emotional intelligence quotient, which determines how well you relate to other people, your ability to put yourself in another's shoes, and how you build rapport. Many people believe that your success in life depends on how well you connect with people. Daniel Goleman (1995) asserts that intellect and emotions are inextricably intertwined. One cannot be developed without the other.

Educating the emotions may be as important as educating the intellect.

But of course, this requires self-awareness. Self-awareness is the ability to manage impulsivity and emotions. It's a willingness to empathize, and it generally requires well-developed social skills. It is the most basic form of intelligence. If building self-awareness is neglected, inadequacies may cause people to fall short of developing fuller intellectual capacities.

Kian, the self-awareness you have at such a young age astounds me. These letters have allowed me to reflect on, record, and celebrate your social-emotional development in the first twenty-three months of your life. As I've shared previously, I have witnessed you observing, exploring, playing, interacting, and experimenting with other people. Every day, you increasingly understand and control your own emotions. You also—as your enjoyment of *The Muppet Movie* reveals—have an increasing awareness of what others might be feeling or thinking.

All of this seems to suggest that you are ever more aware that you are an individual. Consequently, you have started expressing a desire to be more independent. It's natural now for you to want to do things without help. You are even beginning to say how you feel, yelping "ow!" when you bang up against something, or proudly exclaiming "I did it!" after surmounting a new challenge.

The significance of these first experiences is impossible to overstate. These interactions and discoveries will shape who you are and who you will become. They will also build your understanding of how the world works. The important people in your life—your mom and dad, Nana, other family members, and your daycare friends—are all encouraging you and helping you lay the foundation for a range of social-emotional skills. I have faith that in the years since I've written these letters, you have continued to build upon them, and that you are well acquainted with self-regulation, empathy, turn-taking, and sharing. I have no doubt that you have a plethora of positive relationships with other adults and peers.

As I write today, shortly before Christmas, I am reminded of Charles Dickens' classic story, *A Christmas Carol*. Bob Cratchit, Tiny Tim, and that cruel business tycoon, Ebenezer Scrooge, are the key characters in this timeless story of transformation. Scrooge begins as a heartless, bitter, miserly old geezer, but during a single night's visitation from his former partner, Jacob Marley, and three angels, he suddenly sees the world differently. For him, everything changes, when on Christmas Eve, Scrooge gains a new perspective and finally sees the value of contentment and gratitude, simplicity and freedom, empathy and compassion.

In short, Ebenezer Scrooge begins to *feel*. He's lived for work and hoarding money, but overnight, he sees what really matters when he is finally able *to step into another's shoes and empathize with them.*

Kian, as my declining health and aging seem determined to steal more of my energy and seize more control of my body, I am uplifted daily by your smile and joyful spirit. I am buoyed by the puzzled looks you give me as I struggle to get up off the floor after some playtime with you, or as I fall farther and farther behind during our walks in the neighborhood. Clearly, you are an empathetic young man. Unlike Scrooge, you did not need four ghosts to help you understand the concept of compassion.

Perhaps that is due to your sense of humor. A recent study on this subject was scheduled to be released for September of this year, but was called off because of COVID-19. However, the study found that kids develop a sense of humor by age one. Albert Einstein attributed his brilliant mind to having a childlike sense of humor. Indeed, a number of studies have found an association between humor and intelligence.

Mark Twain apparently agreed. He once said, "Humor is the great thing, the saving thing after all. The minute it crops up, all our hardnesses yield, all our irritations, and resentments flit away, and a sunny spirit takes their place." Humor touches nearly every facet of life. In fact, roughly ninety percent of men and eighty percent of women report that a sense of humor is the most important quality in a partner. It's a crucial feature for leaders, too, and it's even been shown to help cancer patients recover faster. There is no doubt that humor is a life skill that everybody needs.

None of this is news to me. Kian, you have been laughing and flashing the "world's best smile" since your birth. But though I am keenly aware of your ability to laugh and joke, I fret that I myself do not have a fully developed sense of humor. I often seem to lack the ability to perceive the humor in a situation that has others laughing and enjoying themselves. And so, I wonder: Can humor be taught? Is humor an innate or learnable trait?

Fortunately, experts say there is no such thing as a completely humorless individual. Comedy is a fundamental part of human nature. Clearly, there are great benefits to further develop my sense of humor. And so, with a smile on my face, I recall your daily laughter and the words of Emerson: "Unless you try to do something beyond what you have already mastered, you will never grow."

I will continue to strive for a greater sense of humor and continue my appreciation for your spirit and leadership.

Love,

Papa

CHAPTEN ELEVEN
My Gift

Christmas Day, 2020

Dear Kian,

Today is Christmas. For many people, it is a day of celebration. A day of family and friends and tables overflowing with food. It is also a day of gift-giving.

I have two predominant thoughts as I begin to write this letter. The first, appropriately, is about a gift. The second is that this will likely be my last letter, at least for now.

Before I elaborate any further, however, I'd like to talk about oak trees. My lifelong love for oak trees began on the Stanford campus almost seventy years ago. Their beauty and strength have always triggered fond memories and uplifted my spirits.

I've always believed that an oak tree has much in common with a human. Every magnificent oak tree was once only a small, seemingly insignificant acorn, just as every human was once a tiny seed in its mother's womb. Both oak trees and children require sunshine, rain, air, and room to grow. Like the unseen concentric circles inside the tree's trunk, our own human minds build layer upon layer of memories and knowledge. Like an oak tree, whose bark gnarls with age, our skin shrivels and wrinkles as we grow older. We both suffer broken limbs. We also learn to hopefully stand firm in life's strong winds.

Many days this past year, Kian, you and I have taken a walk to the end of our street. We then turn right to head toward the Bay Trail, which overlooks the San Pablo Bay. Just before we enter the pathway, though, there stands a beautiful oak tree. We have passed it often, you and me, on our walks.

Today, Christmas Day, I give you this tree as my gift. Now, before you laugh at what may seem like an absurd offering, hear my proposal. I'd like this to be "our tree," something that will surely outlive both of us. Perhaps we can call it "K and P Oak" for Kian and Papa. Or we might refer to it as our "Family Tree." You, in your infinite creativity, may find a better name.

More important than its moniker is the shared meaning we can find in its presence. Our tree, even as it reaches toward the sky, has roots embedded deeply in the damp soil. Its leaves are illuminated by a bright warm sun that enables its branches to reach even higher. It is that sun and that soil that allow our tree to prosper, reproduce, and find worth in its existence.

As our oak tree illustrates, we all have the need to connect or merge with the world around us. But that need exists alongside a second one: to stand out and be recognized for our uniqueness. Throughout our lives, we struggle to achieve a balance between these two conflicting needs. Even as we seek ways to stand out and be seen, we must reconcile that aspiration with a desire to belong and fit in.

This merging of self and community is essential to growing up, growing down, and growing beyond.

To grow up, for example, we must learn to assume accountability for our actions and take responsibility for ourselves. To grow down, or merge with the world, we must invest in our cultural traditions and commit to those around us by taking responsibility for our families, neighborhoods, and communities. To grow beyond, we must imprint on those around us a piece of ourselves: an image we've created, a skill we're passing on, a value we're sharing, or a gesture of support that allows others to make a leap toward their own personal goals.

Strengthening our connections with the world—above, below, and beyond—energizes us to find a place for ourselves in the hearts and minds of the people who are significant to us—our parents, partners, friends, workmates, and children. Caring for others provides us with the strength to develop an appreciation, not only for those who have invested in us, but also for those different than ourselves.

As you read these letters, you might be well into your journey through adolescence. Being a teenager is one of the toughest jobs in the world. Everything is in transition. Everything is intense. Or perhaps you may be on the brink of adulthood, coping with inconsistences and conflicts. You may be experiencing a desire for independence that is colliding with an aversion to self-reliance and personal responsibility. Undoubtedly, however old you are as you read these letters, you are probably so busy living that you have precious little time for any more of Papa's ramblings!

So I'll conclude my letters now with a few final strategies that may prove useful as you continue to stretch your own branches toward the sun and find the best possible soil to grow roots. Nothing I share guarantees happiness, success, or positive outcomes, but these final strategies for life may prove useful as a sort of travel guide as you navigate the years ahead. Glean from them what you find valuable, Kian, and know that they are offered from a deep desire to see you find joy and meaning in your life.

So, with humility and hope, I give you "Papa's Fundamental Life Strategies."

LIFE STRATEGY #1:
Be yourself.

John Gardner, the first U.S. Secretary of Health, Education, and Welfare, shares a story of sitting adjacent to Martin Luther King, Jr. at a 1967 educational conference where the speaker presented a paper entitled "First, Teach Them to Read." As the speaker concluded, King leaned over to Gardner and said, "First teach them to believe in themselves." King's assertion is full of wisdom: We first have to become convinced that we are good enough as we are before we are able to see what we are capable of achieving.

Kian, it has taken me most of my life to learn this invaluable lesson: who we are—our sense of identity—needs to come before what we do. As American author and educator Parker J. Palmer put it, "Before I can tell my life what I want to do with it, I must listen to my life telling me who I am." In other words, we should ask ourselves "who" we are, before we decide "what" we want to do in this life.

Admittedly, I myself skipped the "who" question and jumped right into the "what" question. Like so many others in the world today, I often got so busy with my life's activities—education, career, and family issues—that I completely overlooked the "who" question. You can learn from my mistakes, though. I hope and pray that you are able to recognize that "being" before "doing" is an important—and perhaps necessary—first step to living.

But how do you do that? How do you find answers to that all-important question, "Who am I?" Like our oak tree, we all need to be seen and celebrated as wholly unique selves so that we can be energized by our experiences. But we also need the nourishment that can only come through establishing roots. This includes developing an appreciation for the cultural context that surrounds us, and that includes our classmates, friends, mentors, family, and even strangers whose paths cross ours. These relationships can uplift our spirits and inform our decisions. Your uniqueness, Kian, resides in the ways you integrate and use what you learn from others to direct your life's choices. Then you are emboldened to express yourself authentically, unafraid to stand out.

LIFE STRATEGY #2:
Keep your expectations in check.

I've never been a fan of expectations. They block our development and limit our horizons. When we have an expectation, we are confident that something will turn out in a particular way. We may be looking forward to it, as if it is due to happen. Meanwhile, however, we are distracted from the moment, and the task at hand. It is then far too easy to become confused, unfocused, pressured, and anxious, all of which interfere with our ability to accomplish what we set out to do. When we do not tie ourselves to expectations or preconceived notions, we can better see, understand, and enjoy ourselves and our lives.

Kian, I firmly believe when we put aside expectations and accept that we can't control everything, we will find that our relationships, careers, and futures become open to endless and empowering possibilities. One way to do this is to focus on the direction in which your feet are headed at the moment, and then establish a purpose instead of an expectation. A purpose indicates you have less concern for the outcome. This helps you direct your efforts toward the best possible outcome while keeping yourself open to greater possibilities, instead of limiting yourself with defined expectations.

LIFE STRATEGY #3:
Identify and accept responsibility.

Kian, it's been a lot of fun to watch you drop one of your balls into your toddler-sized basketball hoop. It's also brought back some fond memories of the many years that basketball was a cornerstone of my life.

As I write this, I remember the unique way one basketball coach, Les Yellin, summarized the main qualities and virtues of a player in the form of acronyms. He referred to them as "IQ," "EQ," and "RQ."

IQ, or Intelligence Quotient, means what it always means: the function of intelligence. Behaving intelligently is knowing what a smart player should do on the basketball court.

EQ stands for Energy Quotient, or having the energy to work at what you are doing. When your EQ is good, you practice harder, play the game better, and find ways to keep moving despite being tired or discouraged or defeated.

RQ refers to Responsibility Quotient. It is the ability to know what to do (IQ), to have the energy to do it (EQ), but also to understand that whatever it is, it must be done. We are all likely to do the things we want to do well. But there are also those things we may not want to do but have to do, and *those* things, too, must be done well. Kian, my philosophy is always to do what I have to do, and if it turns out that it's also something I *want* to do, that's just icing on the cake. When we learn what we have to do and do it, that's our RQ.

Understanding RQ as a fundamental life strategy enables us to experience life at a more fulfilling level. Integrating the spirit of responsibility into our daily thinking and behaviors makes a difference in our feelings of

self-satisfaction. I would wholeheart-
edly encourage you to embrace responsibility instead of avoiding it.

LIFE STRATEGY #4:
Look forward.

Kian, the choices you will make
each day will shape your future. Every
situation will provide you with opportunities to do things that make a positive difference in your life, or, con-
versely, become things you may end up
regretting.

The old adage, "Life is short,"
would not have resonated with me when
I was your age. However, we can all
learn something from the 1988 classic
movie *Dead Poets Society*. On the first
day of class, Mr. Keating, the new En-
glish teacher, takes his class of twen-
ty-five boys out into the hall to look
at old black-and-white photos of the
young men who attended the school,
Welton Academy, more than a half cen-
tury earlier.

Employing unorthodox teaching
methods, Keating urges the students to
lean in and listen closely to the whis-
pers of the former students as he whis-

pers in their ears, "Car-pe, Car-pe, Carpe diem. Seize the day, boys! Make your lives extraordinary!" Life is indeed short. Take every opportunity that each day offers you.

Over the course of your life, you will see and do things you can't even imagine right now. Your frame of reference may be currently limited to what is known or tangible, or what you have experienced thus far in your life. But life is full of change. The transitions, when they come, won't be easy. You'll find yourself adapting to a new way of life, only to meet a new challenge, which then precipitates more change. It is in these moments, when you are pushed outside of your comfort zone, that you have the opportunity to learn and grow the most. So, as difficult and daunting as they may seem, seek out these opportunities. Your life will be better for it.

There's an old and familiar Buddhist saying, "When the student is ready, the teacher will appear." Kian, you have been the teacher for the past two years, and I your willing student throughout this rich and meaningful journey. This has been a time that has challenged both of us; me in the winter of my life, and you in the spring of yours. We are both having to take care of ourselves by staying active physically and mentally. Despite our tremendous difference in age, we are continuing to grow and learn, to listen to our inner voices, and to commit to meaningful self-development. We are also finding ways to respect ourselves, hold ourselves in high self-esteem. And we are giving to our communities by sharing our life experiences and helping others. We will continue to find meaning in our lives through love, faith, friendship, self-forgiveness, identity, happiness, and success.

I hope these letters have conveyed that you are not alone. I also hope that they have provided you with some new awareness and knowledge that bring meaning and joy to your journey.

I leave you with a final thought, one that has been echoed by spiritual teachers over the centuries: Happiness comes from helping others. Connection is what gives life meaning.

When you pass by our oak tree, perhaps you will remember this and know how my connection to you has brought both happiness and meaning to my life.

Love you,

Papa

AUTHOR'S NOTE:
TO GRANDPARENTS

January 2021

Dear Fellow Grandparents,

A Cree elder from Canada once shared a final conversation he'd had with his aging grandfather. "Grandfather," he asked, "What is the meaning of life?" After a period of thought, the old man answered, "Grandson, children are the purpose of life. We were once young and someone cared for us, and now it is our time to care."

The heart of this story—conveyed through the letters I've written to my two-year-old grandson Kian—is the many ways in which he has taken care of me. But writing this has also given me the unexpected opportunity to reflect on what it means to be a grandparent.

It may seem obvious, but I've realized through the process of writing these letters and observing Kian that I have a choice about how I interact with my grandchildren. Though not always easy, given this aging and ailing body of mine, I have always sought to be positive, encouraging, and caring. I have also cherished the opportunity to help my grandchildren feel more self-responsible, competent, and independent, so that they can become people who feel comfortable in their own skin.

Nearly every grandparent wants the kind of relationship with their grandchildren that we see in Hallmark commercials: loving and warm, and full of mutual respect. In reality, the grandparent-grandchild bond, while special, can be strained by distance, vastly different values, or in some cases, the need for the grandparent to fill the role of the parent. I won't pretend to know all the challenges that grandparents face today, but I would love to offer a few observations from my own grandparenting journey.

First, I've learned the importance of being real. After a lifetime of working as a pastor and psychologist, as well as a coach to athletes and business leaders, and the founder of a non-profit youth leadership development program, I am convinced that being real is essential to helping our grandchildren see the world both as it is and as it can be. Authenticity builds trust. Trust then creates confidence. Confidence enables people to think beyond what is in front of them; in other words, it allows them to take risks and affect change.

Though not always easy, I found that being real around Kian and my other grandchildren brought us closer. Children are naturally attuned to detect when someone is being fake or phony, and it almost always creates an unease or distrust in them. They want us to be authentic. They want to see the adults in their lives grapple with challenges in front of them, to sweat when the work is hard, to admit when we don't know something, and to show emotion.

My years of experience and the different roles I've had professionally have also helped me gain an understanding and an appreciation for how children learn. Our grandchildren learn exponentially more by observing and by doing, as opposed to being told what to do or not to do. Educator John Holt believed that young people "do not need to be made to learn." Indeed, children are born with what Einstein called "the holy curiosity of inquiry." If we can unleash their curiosity, or better yet, *encourage* it, we will have a front-row seat to witness their boundless imagination and limitless acquisition of knowledge.

I have also chosen to try to see every interaction with my grandchildren as a gift. Years ago, I read about the complicated and intricate steps of the Japanese tea ceremony. I was mystified. What was the big deal about laying utensils out in a specific order? But when I learned that the purpose of the careful attention to detail is to remind us that we can never take anything for granted—especially the people we care about—I suddenly understood the importance of the ceremony.

A day will come when we meet with a loved one for the last time. Since we don't know when that is, we should attempt to treat every encounter as if it were indeed a once-in-a-lifetime occurrence. We should act as if we may never get another chance to connect and communicate our love for them. We should seek to benefit as much as possible from the gifts they inherently give us.

In nearly all of the letters I've written to Kian, I've shared things I've observed him doing. Observing our grandchildren, just watching them play and interact, is one of the simplest ways we can come to know them better! As author Henry James advised, "Observe perpetually." The ability to patiently and intently observe our grandchildren is one of the most rewarding skills we can develop. True observation involves sensitivity, compassion, and keen listening. Admittedly, it takes a lot of practice. But as I learned to observe Kian, I gradually came to understand why he behaved as he did. Observing him was an essential part of being his Papa.

So often, children communicate a great deal through their behavior. By watching them, we can learn what their strengths are—how they are naturally friendly or genuinely empathetic. We can identify what they need from us and from others—a comforting hug, an encouraging nod, a firmer boundary. We can also begin to identify clues about why they misbehave—exhaustion, discomfort, a desire for attention. By learning to truly observe our grandchildren, we can discover who they are, what motivates them, and what worries them—information that helps connect us and build a more meaningful relationship with these amazing young people.

The partner to keen observation is reflection. Reflection directs us to put aside our own feelings and contemplate what the child is thinking and feeling; to consider their point of view. It's a way of showing that we truly understand them, or at the very least, that we want to! Reflection naturally puts us in our grandchildren's shoes, where we try to understand their experiences better. The goal is to listen for their feelings and thoughts and find a way to mirror them back. Hopefully the child then recognizes that they have been heard and understood, and in doing so, we validate their feelings and strengthen their confidence in themselves.

Reflection also builds their confidence and trust in us. When we reflect, we say to our grandchild: "Even when you are mad or don't want to do what you've been asked, I'm willing to hear you out. I care about you." Once they sense our genuine interest and compassion, they're more open to hearing what we have to say.

Over my lifetime, I've truly come to understand how important reflection can be. Not surprisingly, metacognition—awareness of our own thought processes—is a key part of emotional and cognitive growth, and a valuable tool to help our grandchildren learn. Plato said, "When the mind is thinking it is talking to itself." The ability to think about and regulate their own thoughts can help our grandchildren not only find greater success—but happiness. So, as a grandparent, this means that my goal is not to teach my grandchildren what to think, but to help them learn how to think.

Maria Montessori, the famous Italian physician and educator, wrote extensively about how young children literally soak up everything in their environment, including the behaviors and attitudes of the significant adults in their lives. She called this unique way of learning the "absorbent mind." In other words, what we tell our grandchildren is far less important than who we are. Similarly, the psychoanalysis Carl Jung advised, "If there is anything we wish to change in the child, we should first examine it and see whether it is not something that could better be changed in ourselves." I believe both doctors—Montessori and Jung—are suggesting that to be the best grandparents we can be, we should visit our own values, beliefs, strengths, and weaknesses to engage in a process of self-reflection before we judge the grandchildren we care about most.

And of course, we do care about them, and they need to know this. Caring is a process in which we selflessly help the people near us—our grandchildren, for one—grow and actualize themselves through our attention and commitment. Caring requires qualities such as patience, trust, honesty, and courage. Additionally, to care requires us to hone our listening skills, to respond with gentleness and understanding, and to offer warmth and encouragement. Overall, it means loving our grandchildren in such a way that demonstrates how much we care about them and enjoy being their grandparent. I want Kian and his cousins to always know that they are understood, respected, and cared for by another person.

Because I care, my thoughts whirl with concerns for Kian and today's youth. I hope to continue to learn how, as a grandfather, I can be there for my grandchildren as they face life's challenges on their journeys toward adulthood. Surely, they will encounter many of the same challenges that we faced in our lives. They will grapple with questions and insecurities as they search for meaning and purpose. They will struggle to set aside time for the stillness, silence, and solitude that they need to strengthen their identities and set their own goals. They will hunger for joy and delight and search for ways to be creative. They will seek nurturing relationships and meaningful connections with people and groups. They will long to belong. They will try to make a difference.

We can't always smooth the path ahead for them. But we can—by being authentic, by observing and seeking to understand them, by reflecting on our time with them, and by helping them reflect on themselves— be the best grandparents we can be and hope our relationship brings them great satisfaction.

As Plutarch put it: The mind is not a vessel to be filled but a fire to be kindled. Our grandchildren are not vessels that you and I—as grandparents—should strive to fill. Instead, they are waiting for a spark to set them aglow. As grandparents, we have the unique opportunity to be that spark.

With deep regards,

George Selleck—Kian's Grandfather

ACKNOWLEDGMENTS:
MEMORIES, REGRETS, AND FILLING THE GAPS

First, To My Grandchildren:

The six months it has taken me to write the letters compiled in this book, *Kian and Me: Gifts from a Grandson*, have been an enlightening personal journey, to say the least. I have spent many hours pondering the past and reflecting about times we've shared, recalling some of my favorite memories, and acknowledging the miles that have sometimes separated us. It is difficult not to regret those times I was not with you more, and I wish that life had not cheated us out of more shared experiences.

This book—these letters—are specifically about my experiences with Kian. Yet in a very real sense, they are about the meaning I've found in my interactions with all of you, as well as the deep joy that my heart holds for each of you. I like to think that if you had been born within walking distance of my home, as Kian was, and that the circumstances of my health and aging had removed me from my ongoing work as they have now, we too may have built a similar story—one chronicling a companion journey starting on the day you entered this world and leading up to the week before your second birthday.

I'd also like to think that the many rich and unique experiences I shared with each of you were the foundation and essential learning I needed to be present and available to Kian. From my first days of knowing each one of you—Alexis, Jessica, Spencer, Kennedy, Kai, Aiden, and Rowan—with your diverse interests, intelligent and curious minds, playful spirits, and your sensitive and loving hearts, you have given my life meaning and joy and prepared me to be the best grandfather I could be for your cousin Kian.

With each new letter that I wrote, I became increasingly and firmly convinced that my experiences with all of you and this culminating time with Kian are no doubt the final—but easily the best—chapter in my lifelong search for a family.

During each day I spent with Kian, I was reminded constantly of all of you. Though it was his hand I was able to hold, I would wonder what all of you were doing. I was reminded often of our precious moments, with flashes of regret that I never had the same time to spend with you that I had with him.

Still, I am grateful to have many special memories of watching each of you, spending time with you, talking with you, and listening to you. I think of Alexis and Jessica teaming up to whip me in Monopoly. I can picture, just like it was yesterday, joining you and your dad in that school parking lot when you first learned to ride a bike. I remember the many times that we would grab a bite to eat together at one of your favorite Berkeley restaurants. With a smile, I can see you both cheering me on at the Stanford alumni basketball game.

And Spencer, I so loved playing catch with you! It made me incredibly proud to sit in the stands at your baseball games. Your frequent phone calls, during which you inevitably provided your latest thoughts on the politics of the day, were and will continue to be a highlight for me. But even just a trip to McDonalds with you, for your favorite Egg & Cheese McGriddles, of course, made for a special time together.

Kennedy and Kai, how I loved cheering you on at whatever sport was on the docket that weekend: volleyball, soccer, or baseball. Do you remember the hide-and-seek games in your home? You could never find me! I cherish that time with both of you: our trips to Hawaii, the afternoons swimming in your pool, or sharing meals with you and your family.

Ever-curious Aiden, what fun memories I have of your sleepovers. And no matter how many Facetimes I've shared with you and your Nana and Rowan, you always have a welcome smile for your Papa. It tickles me to see your engineer's inquisitiveness, and I am absolutely positive that your younger brother who turns one this week holds the record for the fastest crawler on the planet!

To my adopted grandkids, Christian, Cayleb, and Cara, you are never far from my thoughts and prayers. You are incredibly special to me.

These memories I have of us—seemingly mundane and ordinary—are priceless. My biggest regret is that we have not shared more time together and made more memories. Please know that my respect and love for each of you is ever-present and knows no bounds.

To Every Member of My Family:

As a young boy, I grew up in Compton, California—not too far outside of Los Angeles. I had an unquenchable passion for sports. I'll refrain from re-telling my entire athletic journey, except to say something that was essential to pretty much any sport, and especially the sport I loved most, basketball: teamwork. Teamwork—or maybe, more precisely, synergy—is the thing that I think most encapsulates the heart of our family. While we are scattered across this vast country, with some of us even living abroad, I like to think that we are still connected—never apart for long in our thoughts of each other, in our concerns for one another, and in our eagerness to catch up and be together again.

Though this book and these letters have centered on my journey as a grandfather, I would not be on this journey were it not for my three remarkable children: John, Alison, and Peter Selleck. Though Alison passed away in 2007, there is not a day that I don't think of the three of you and feel gratitude for all of you. Just as Kian has given me countless gifts, so have each of you. You've nurtured and taught me how to be a father. You've modeled patience and wisdom through your own parenting and relationships. And mostly, you've loved me into being the person I have become in the winter of my life. You have inspired me far beyond what you know.

You've also raised five remarkable grandchildren, each of whom is a gift to me, and dare I say, to the world. You've set aside time to spend with them, and you've given them the attention they deserved and needed, something I wish I had done a better job of myself. I know well the challenge of balancing parenthood with a career, and I marvel at how well each of you have tackled that challenge. All of you, along with your spouses, have modeled what it truly means to be a parent.

John, Tomasa, and Kathlyn: I have watched and been buoyed by the support you show your girls, how you have encouraged their wonderful artistic sides, championed their deep intellectual interests, and set them up to embrace the adventures ahead of them.

Peter and Jenny: Your profound respect for the emotions of your two children is inspiring. I remember when Kennedy was about Kian's age, or maybe a little older. I don't remember exactly what the behavior was, but as we—Jenny, Peter, and I—watched her play in the center of your tiny apartment's front room, she did something that necessitated a consequence. Kennedy quickly burst into tears. Both of you rushed in to embrace her and reassure that she was precious and loved. Almost immediately, her sobbing stopped. Having comforted her, you both backed away to your original locations, after which Jenny proceeded with the consequence by saying firmly but gently to Kennedy, "Are you ready now for your time-out?" You put her emotions first and then addressed the behavior.

Alison and Keith: Both of you are sorely missed. You gave your only child the strength, courage, and ability to strike out on his own, overcome challenges, and build a life for himself that you would surely be incredibly proud of.

Domonic and Amanda: Your journey as parents is just beginning, and yet already, your desire to be the best ones possible is evident in the way you seek to understand the reasons behind your children's behavior rather than just react to it. I admire the time, energy, and love you are pouring into raising your boys.

All of you have wisely chosen not to create paths for your children. Instead, you are showing them the support and encouragement they need to allow them to create their own paths. There are few things more rewarding than seeing your own children become the nurturing, authentic, compassionate parents all of you are.

And finally, I'd like to acknowledge Kian's parents: Matt and Kathy Collins. Quite simply, you are incredible parents. I can't imagine anything more you could do or be for Kian that would help him develop any better. In addition to your consistent and naturally loving behavior, you have shown such thought and taken great care to be the best parents you can. Your constant attention to every detail and your commitment to do what's best for Kian fills my heart with hope, gratitude, and love.

It may be a bit of a stretch, but the words of the boxer Rocky Balboa in the movie *Rocky* capture the sentiment I have for our family. He describes the relationship that exists between himself and his girlfriend, whose personality is so different from his. "I've got gaps, she's got gaps," Rocky says. "But together we've got no gaps." While I can't truthfully say we have no gaps—every family does—I think we do an admirable job of shoring them up when they arise!

It's my greatest hope that as each of you read through these letters—and I hope you do read them at some point—you find enjoyment in them and perhaps are reminded of something you and I shared once, one of the many dances of life that I was honored enough to take with you. I also hope that you take well-deserved credit for the many lessons you have taught me.

Finally, but most importantly, as you continue your own beautiful dances of life, and as you move along your journey toward adulthood and parenthood and eventually being a grandparent, promise me that you will fill in for me in my absence.

I pray, too, that even as years and miles separate us physically, we will always work—as a team—to keep our gaps small and manageable.